Summary

A story from the perspective of a Roti - that is really fun and creative. It is a mix of humour, a little suspense, and lots of imagination. Here is a short playful story for kids. The story is light hearted and positive.I am sure you would be curious about the roti Raman. Enjoy reading!

Raman enjoys his massages.

Raman is now being pressed.
So that he becomes a thin
flat circle.

As Raman was placed on the griddle, he felt the warmth rise.

But soon, he felt himself
start to bubble.

His edges started to lift off
the griddle, and he puffed up
like a little balloon.

Raman is scared of hot griddles.

But Raman felt it like a gentle, warm embrace. Just like being hugged by the sun.

But just as quickly as the joy came, it was time for the flip. Roti Raman was tossed in the air.

Raman could already hear the sound of his delicious, crispy, golden surface.

Raman is now excited about meeting his new friends.

Roti Raman was dipped in curry and torn apart with warm hands. But he realized, it wasn't so bad being cooked.

Being the perfect roti for someone's meal is Raman's happiness.

Roti Raman loved resting and relaxing in the lunch box.

Roti Raman lived on in every tummy he touched. He is a little hero in every meal

Every little bite told a story
of warmth, love and happiness.

Raman is a happy Roti.

Do you like Raman, The Roti

?